Simply Elfje

Elizabeth Leaper is a poet, writer and blogger. Her work has appeared in several anthologies and small press magazines as well as various online sites. She has previously published two poetry collections and a children's story book, which is an updated version of a story that was first broadcast on BBC Radio in the 1970's.

For Children

Barking at Nothing (a collection of verse)
The Thirsty Flowers (illustrated story book)

Poetry

Collecting Cobwebs, Gathering Brambles
(with Jack Williamson)

Elizabeth Leaper

Simply Elfje

little poems in just eleven words

Silverburn Publishing

Simply Elfje
is dedicated to all those writers
who have shared the Elfje journey with me.

The net profits from the sale of this book
will be donated to charity.

First published in 2017
by Silverburn Publishing
www.silverburnpublishing.co.uk

ISBN: 978-0-9547010-4-8

Contents

Introduction

Simply Elfje started life as a blog with the aim of bringing this fascinating short form poetry to a wider audience. The Elfje poetic short form originated in The Netherlands, where it was developed as a tool for teaching young children about writing poetry and it was not widely known away from these roots.

The name Elfje translates from the Dutch as 'elfin' or 'fairy' poem. I am often asked how to pronounce the word and the best approximation I can give you is *ell-fyer*. The form consists of just eleven words spread over five lines and there is an obvious connection between the words 'elfin' and 'eleven' that I am sure the reader will recognise!

I was introduced to the form some four years ago by a friend who lives in The Netherlands. It was then that I began the *Simply Elfje* blog. Although it is no longer regularly updated the blog can still be found at http://simplyelfje.wordpress.com if you wish to take a look.

These little elfin poems share similarities with two other short forms of poetry, the Haiku and the Cinquain; the main difference being that these two forms are based on syllable count whereas the Elfje is based on word count. This makes it easier for young children to understand and shape their own poems. Like these two other forms, especially the Haiku, the Elfje should also end with that undefinable moment, the 'wow' factor, which in this case is referred to as 'the bomb'.

As with Haiku it is not necessary for Elfje to have a title. Having said that the poems in this book are titled. For the purposes of the blog it was easier for them to be identified in this way and it made sense to carry those titles over into the book.

Within these pages I have chosen to present many of my own Elfje that have appeared on the blog over the four year period of its life, plus a selection of those that I have written more recently. As well as sharing my own experiments with the form other writers were invited to submit Elfje for inclusion on the blog and a selection of these are also represented here.

I gave much thought as to how best to present these little poems and finally decided that, as much of the subject matter is seasonal this was as good a way as any for sharing them. Those poems that do not easily fit these seasonal divisions have their own section. The single Elfje at the bottom of each title page has been specially chosen to sum up the theme of that section.

The final section of the book, *Other Words*, is reserved for the guest contributors. These have been presented in alphabetical order according to the individual writer's names. Where several Elfje are by the same writer the name appears just once on a page, to the right of the verse, and the writer should be understood to have written all that follows until a new writer's name appears.

The aim of the book is to continue to promote this fascinating and fun short form. It is a book for dipping into rather than reading from cover to cover and I hope you enjoy dipping into these pages where perhaps you will find inspiration for your own experiments with the Elfje form.

Elizabeth Leaper   March 2017

How to Write an Elfje

Elegant
Little verse
Following simple rules,
Just eleven words long.
Elfje.

My Elfje Acrostic above summarises the simple rules which are explained more fully below.

An Elfje consists of five sentences written in five lines:

Line 1 is just one word. This word symbolises a colour or feature and creates the atmosphere of the poem.

Line 2 has two words that tell you something about this colour or feature, a clue as to what it is, whether it is a person or an object.

Line 3. Three words giving more information about the person or the object. You describe where or who the person or the object is, or what the person or object is doing. This sentence often, but not always, starts with the word 'he', 'she' or 'it.'

Line 4 is four words long. You are writing something about yourself in relation to the person or the object. It gives the final piece of information. It is your conclusion.

Line 5. One word to finish. This word is called the 'Bomb', it is the 'wow' factor. It sums up the essence of the poem.

It is not necessary to give your Elfje a title although in this book, for reasons explained in the Introduction, they do have titles. You could simply call yours 'Elfje' if you prefer.

Here is an example of one of my own Elfje that more or less follows the rules:

Blue.   (the colour)
The sky.   (the 'what')
Above my head.   (the 'where')
No clouds in sight.   (more information/conclusion)
Hot.   (the 'bomb')

However, as you write your Elfje you will find that to slavishly follow the rules can be rather restricting and the result seem unpoetic, so why not bend them a bit? Most of the Elfje in this book will have done so to some degree. When you write your own read them through to make sure they flow nicely and try, if possible, to avoid ending a line with a weak word such as 'a'. This won't work well as the opening word either! You can let the lines flow on but please keep to the eleven word count and be sure to check that there is a satisfying 'bomb' at the end.

Spring

Winter Retreats

Cold
winter retreats.
Through the darkness
new growth bursts announcing
spring.

Before Time

Pearly
half-moon,
up before time,
watches the setting sun
blush.

————————

Tulips

Red
tulips reach
towards the sky,
petals raised, drinking in
sunshine.

————————

Burning Bush

Blazing
Pieris buds,
fiery finger tips
like Moses' burning bush
aflame.

————————

Paint

Magical
colourful arc,
Nature's paint palette,
sweeps across the sky.
Rainbow.

In Your Face

Bold,
brash, brassy,
in your face,
full of spring bling:
daffodils.

———————

Crab-Apple Blossom

Crab
Apple blossom,
pink sugar tutus,
ballerinas waiting to start
dancing.

———————

Return

Bare
trees sprout
new buds. Colour
returns to the garden.
Spring.

———————

Neighbour's Tree

Magnificent
magnolia blossom
on neighbour's tree.
Beauty over the garden
fence.

Pompoms

Cherry
blossom pompoms,
delicate lacy clusters
threaded along the branches,
rejoicing.

————

Horizons

Changing
the view,
fresh green leaves
cover bare branches, hiding
horizons.

————

Patchwork

Dappled
patchwork shadows
on the lawn.
Sunlight filtered through the
trees.

————

Indignation

Acrobatic
squirrel stealing
from bird feeders.
Indignant blue-tit approaches, watches,
retreats.

Mystery

Air
of mystery,
the pale moon
wearing clouds like a
veil.

————

Between Trees

Glimpsed
between trees
from upstairs window,
glistening rooftops wet with
rain.

————

Shower

Lifting
each wing
into the rain,
taking his morning shower –
Pigeon.

————

Breeze Blown

Breeze
blown blooms,
delicate yellows, bright
reds, vibrant blues; colourful
spring.

Light

Sun
in daytime.
Moon at night.
Even in our darkness,
light.

————

Wisteria

So
many years
the Wisteria has
never flowered, but look –
buds!

————

Flying

Clear
blue sky,
straight line contrails.
People flying to warmer
climes.

————

Equinox

Day
and night
of equal length.
Everything now in balance.
Equinox.

Summer

Promise

Sun
at last
in the garden.
Time for summer's glorious
promise.

Sapphire Dart

Iridescent
sapphire dart,
translucent, intangible, ephemeral,
flashes across my vision –
dragonfly.

––––––––

June

June.
Wettest since
records first began.
Rivers, lakes and reservoirs
replenished.

––––––––

Sing

Blue,
the sky
between the clouds,
uplifting, making my heart
sing.

––––––––

Infinity

Vast
the skies
around the boat.
My soul expands into
infinity.

Rowan Berries

Red
Rowan berries,
Mountain Ash tree
so sacred to Celtic
mythology.

———

Come and Go

Sunshine,
intermittent showers
come and go
creating our lush green
land.

———

Lethargy

Humid,
lethargic day.
Charity shop books
tempt me to start
reading.

———

Believe

Above
the clouds,
hidden from view,
wall to wall sunshine.
Believe.

Dawn

Dawn
light creeps
through my window
with a hint of
sunshine.

———————

Birdsong

Birdsong
and sunshine.
On the bench
I sit, eyes closed,
listening.

———————

Pink Roses

Late.
At last
pink roses bloom
against the garden fence.
Delight.

———————

Sunrise

'Sunrise'
climbing rose,
bright orange with
a hint of pink –
beautiful.

Cosmos

Bees
cluster around
the bright white
flowers of the Cosmos,
feasting.

————

Filtered

Sun
weakly filtered
through soft clouds
makes a cooler day.
Relief.

————

Breeze

Still
the air,
yet treetop leaves
flutter in an unseen
breeze.

————

Oppressive

Intense,
oppressive stillness,
air pressure builds.
The calm before the
storm.

After

After
rain, sun
briefly peers through
the last hour of
daylight.

————

Brush Stokes

Watercolour
brush strokes
paint the lowering
cloud formations and crimson
sunset.

————

Storm

Thunder
crashing, lightning
flashing, storm-darkened
sky, livid as a
bruise.

————

Wet

Wet
and dismal
change in weather.
When will summer days
return?

Autumn

Seesaw

Time
flies by.
Seesaw has tipped.
Days sliding away towards
autumn.

Leaves

Green,
the leaves
on the trees,
turning red and gold.
Autumn.

———

Over

Holiday
now over.
No more sun.
Nothing but grim, grey
rain.

———

Morning Mist

Early
morning mist,
depressing damp drizzle.
The changing face of
autumn.

———

Pumpkin Face

Round
pumpkin face
of the moon,
arrived for Halloween too
soon.

Misty

Misty
autumn morning,
magical veil between
worlds, for those who
look.

————

Freedom

Making
a bid
for freedom, leaves
leap into the dancing
breeze.

————

Unadorned

Bare
boned trees
begin to show
elegant simplicity of form
unadorned.

————

Between the Storms

Hush,
the air
is calm, still.
How long will it
last?

Ebb and Flow

Sunshine
and showers,
the seasons come
and go, ebb and
flow.

Cloud Cover

Misty
and mystical
clouds cover the
tops of the Yorkshire
moors.

Harvest

Fruits
and berries
coming to ripeness –
harvest produce for winter
feasts.

Suddenly

Rain
clouds clear.
Suddenly blue sky
allows bright evening sunshine.
Glorious.

Strong Winds

Strong
winds sweep
through the trees.
Innocent blue skies follow.
Stillness.

————————

Wind

Wind
sighing mournfully
around the boats
rocking gently in the
marina.

————————

Change

Leaves
turn gold
as days shorten,
nights lengthen and seasons
change.

————————

Clocks

Clocks
go back.
Night comes earlier.
Holly King claims his
kingdom.

Changes

Autumn
presses on.
Mild October ends.
November rolls in bringing
changes.

———————

Naked

When
I return
I will see
stark winter trees stripped
naked.

———————

Singing

Singing
his song,
memories of spring
in warm autumn sunshine.
Robin.

———————

Misty Mornings

Misty
mornings tell
their own tale –
summer days drifting into
autumn.

Winter

Snow

White,
the lawn,
like iced cake.
First of the winter
snow.

Evening

Cold
and still.
In fading light
Evening draws her cloak
tightly.

____

Mince Pies

Mince
Pies baking
in the oven.
Treats for the Christmas
season.

____

First Footing

First
footing with
lump of coal,
bringing in the New
Year.

____

Robin

Robin
red-breast,
always first to
check out the bird
feeders.

Winter Fun

Gliding
on sledges
down the hill.
Winter fun in the
snow.

————

Snowfall

Just
when we
think the thaw
is coming, more snow
falls.

————

Overflow

Rain
and melted
snow with nowhere
to go. Rivers overflow.
Floods.

————

Warmth

White
snowdrop buds,
heads coyly bowed,
enjoy the weak sun's
warmth.

Sky

Here
and there
amongst grey cloud
illusive patches of blue
sky.

————

Cusp

Janus,
looking both
backwards and forwards –
cusp of the New
Year.

————

Washed Away

Wind
and rain.
Old year washed
away. A fresh new
beginning.

————

Full

Back
home it's
February Fill-Dyke,
but the dykes are
full!

Relentless

Close
the curtains,
shut it out –
the relentless wind and
rain.

———

Washout

As
winters go,
this one has
been something of a
washout.

———

Landscape

Cold
and still,
frost-coated landscape
gripped by stark winter's
beauty.

———

Holly

Holly
branches laden.
Bright red berries
decorate our home this
Yuletide.

Solstice

Holly
is king.
Night and day
in balance. Scales soon
tilt.

———————

Father Time

Another
New year.
Old Father Time
ticks on by without
rest.

———————

Without Warmth

Biting
cold blue,
the sky. Sun
shines without warmth. North
wind.

———————

Smoke

Grey
smoke rises
through cold air.
Around the hearth below,
warmth.

Anytime

Ripples

Ripples
on pond
expanding ever outwards
from the small stone's
splash.

Fog

Fog.
No, not
the pea-soupers
of old but veiled
mystery.

————

Dark

Dark,
silky smooth,
rich and seductive,
melts in your mouth.
Chocolate.

————

Water

Water,
life-giving,
sweet, vital, refreshing.
The thirsty earth drinks.
Rain.

————

Times Past

Horse
brasses hang
beside the fire.
Symbols of times past.
Nostalgia.

Blank Page

Blank
the page,
pristine before me.
What will I write
today?

———————

Days

Days,
tomorrow, today,
come and go,
swiftly passing into yesterday,
history.

———————

Stones

Stones,
what secrets
do you hide?
Are you best left
unturned?

———————

Peace

Practising
Tai Chi
on the lawn
I find inner silence,
peace.

Spider Woman

Spider
Woman weaves
the life weft
across the warp of
time.

————

Fur

Soft,
her fur
beneath my hand.
I feel my cat
purr.

————

Technology

Whole
new meaning
to Raspberry Pie!
Technological jargon hijacks our
language.

————

Clouds

Sky:
blue. Clouds:
one or two
(white, puffy, fluffy) scurry
by.

Writer's Block

Words
swirl around
my head but
none fall onto the
page.

————

Moonshine

Clouds
sweep across
the moon, polishing
her face until it
shines.

————

Life

Web
of life
connects all things.
Invisible threads vibrate in
harmony.

————

The Old Ones

Hidden
from view
the Old Ones
draw closer through the
mist.

Squirrel

Squirrel
pauses warily
on fence post,
flees into ash tree.
Gone.

————

Repaired

Repaired,
the clock
ticks and chimes,
mellow, sonorous, rich and
comforting.

————

Weaving

Weaving
the weft
side to side
through the strong warp
threads.

————

Sea

Designing
for weaving –
a little yacht
tossed on a stormy
sea.

Eyes

Throw
the stick…
please. My daughter's
dog pleads with his
eyes.

————

Between Showers

Walking
the dog,
avoiding the puddles,
keeping ourselves dry between
showers.

————

Warping

Warping
the frame
loom. Getting ready
to weave a new
design.

————

Challenge

Swinging
bird feeders,
blown by the wind,
presents challenge to garden
birds.

Veneer

Chocolate
Easter Eggs.
Pagan memories stir
under veneer of Christian
festivities.

———————

Mellow

Silence
broken only
by the mellow
chimes of the grandfather
clock.

———————

Garden Report

Garden
Report: weeds
winning the battle.
Aching body must withdraw,
regroup.

———————

Above Water

Head
above water,
bright eyes alert,
watching, seal curious as
me.

Stories

Inland,
wind whispers
through trees stories
brought by waves across
seas.

———

Teasing

Sun
peeps through
clouds, teasing with
promises of better weather
soon.

———

Queueing

One
hundred hearses
at the garage,
queueing for fuel: bad
dream!

———

Evening Meal

Helping
himself to
evening meal left
out for stray cat –
hedgehog.

Flying Free

Lost
purple balloon
flying free, skywards.
Child wails with grief.
Tears.

————

Refilled

Bird
feeders refilled,
starlings gather first,
pigeons queue up behind,
impatient.

————

Keepers

Deep
earth rooted,
reaching ever skyward,
ancient keepers of wisdom.
Trees.

————

Empty Space

Light
shines through
the empty space
where the tree once
stood.

New Elfje

Words

Words
like seeds
scattered on paper
grow into little verses.
Elfje.

Message

Red
rose bud
against the fence.
Message to my heart;
Love.

————

Signal

Green
new leaves
on trees signal
the end of winter.
Spring.

————

Blue Sky

Blue,
the sky
above my head,
clear, crisp and bright.
Frost.

————

Grey Day

Another
grey day.
Damp winter drizzle.
I wear my red
coat.

Fingertips

Deceptive
bright sunshine,
bitterly cold wind.
Winter still hangs on.
Fingertips.

———————

Return

So,
he returns,
scuffling among roots
by the beech tree.
Hedgehog.

———————

Puppets

Puppets
on strings,
pulled this way
and that. Knee-jerk
reaction.

———————

Race

Clouds,
wind-blown,
race each other,
jostling for position, destination
unknown.

Bees

September.
Bright sunshine,
warm as summer.
Bees gather late pollen.
Harvest.

————————

Crafted

Fine
and filigree,
more skilfully crafted
than by human hand.
Cobweb.

————————

Single File

Caught
in headlights,
single file across
the road – three wild
boar.

————————

Snow

Snow
at last,
lying stretched like
a pauper's worn, old,
blanket.

In My Face

White
soft flakes
falling to earth
blow in my face.
Snow.

———————

One, Two, Three

One,
two, three…
round she goes,
music in her head.
Dancing.

———————

Downhill

Downhill
at speed
on my bicycle,
the wind behind me.
Elation.

———————

Debutantes

Welcome
Spring's harbingers.
Heads bowed shyly,
white clad debutantes cluster.
Snowdrops.

Hilltop

Standing
on hilltop,
arms gracefully swirling,
collecting energy from wind;
turbines.

———

Sparkling

Golden
sun shines
with gentle warmth,
melting the sparkling diamond
icicles.

———

First Bite

Crisp
first bite,
juices freely flowing,
tantalising my taste buds.
Apple.

———

View

Eyes
so round.
What a view!
I look and look.
Speechless.

Valentine

Heart
of mine
beats so fast,
hoping you'll be my
Valentine.

———————

Pylons

Pylons
striding across
the green countryside
like giant Earth invaders;
Aliens.

———————

Green Grass

Green,
the grass
beneath my feet.
It tickles my toes.
Barefoot.

———————

Wind Chimes

Listen!
Wind chimes
calling little people
to play in my
garden.

Magic

Under
the earth
magic is stirring.
Mother Nature fulfils her
promise.

————

Breeze

New
leaves rustling,
wind chimes tinkling,
daffodils bowing and curtseying.
Breeze.

————

Silence

Deep
snow blanket,
dark starry night,
silence so nearly absolute,
magical.

————

Storm

Storm,
ice chips
rapid gunfire rattle
shot-blasting my face.
Hail.

Other Words

Elfje from guest contributors

Black   Freya Pickard

black
shapes, fluid,
bold, on white
paper, patterns create language;
Words.

Errand Interrupted   Cheryl Anthony-Sterling

Sunset.
Oh my!
Come see this!
Family emerges to share
Wonder.

————

Element of Surprise   Zoë Basil

White
Popping candy
Explodes on deck.
Snap, crackle and pop.
Hail.

————

Dusty   Nancy Brady

Dusty
Chalk marks
On the sidewalk
I toss a pebble
Hopscotch

————

Again   Michael Erb

Nature,
She changes,
We all know that,
And she will repeat
Seasonally.

Sunset   jEtana deGaia

Can
you tell
this is not
the sunrise I promised?
Sunset.

———————

Magical Moments   Becca Givens

Dreams
Of childhood,
Believable magical moments
Creating inspirations to instil
Aspiration.

———————

Autumn

Transition.
Blossoms fading
Roaming turtle saunters
Acorns falling like raindrops
Autumn.

———————

In Her Eyes   Harshal Gupta

constant
the pain
in her eyes
buried under heart warming
smile.

Feet   Fran Hepburn

Feet,
brown toes
on the earth
red soil, green grass
Reconnected.

————

New Life   Alyson Hurst

Splashes,
two frogs
seen by torchlight
more frogspawn laid daily
Spring.

————

Frogs Call   Kani Ilangovan

Sonorous
frogs call
through deep dark
stars answer in gleaming
light.

————

Books

Books
unveil treasures
explore hidden worlds
revelations of life's wonder
connections.

Love   Nikhil Jain

Love.
Mysterious word
with magical meaning
divine feeling of heart
Unexplained.

————————

Unique

Simple
lonesome boy
different from others
living in this world
Unique.

————————

First of May   Cynthia Jobin

Wildflowers,
homemade basket,
bring to door,
ring, run and hide.
Giggle.

————————

The Ways of Water

Swords
pointing down
from frozen eaves
drip, melt in sun –
icicles!

Autumn Promises   Mieke Kolder

Autumn
holds promises.
Sparkling shining gold,
filling darkening days with
Hope.

————

Tactically Speaking   Helen Jane Merritt

Honesty
is rarely
the best policy
unless tempered by some
tact…

————

Lemon Blooms   Claudia Messelodi

Silky
lemon blooms
great the sun.
On my lively terrace,
brightness.

————

Pain

Acute
penetrating pain
of inevitable loss
wounds turned to glass,
regret.

Moon   Claudia Messelodi

Auburn
bloodstained night,
strokes dripping desires,
hearts melting beneath lunar
eclipse.

———————

All About Her   NanLeah N Mick

Panther
Ebony fur
Waiting her turn
Brushing my hair, then
Hers.

———————

Jubilant

Jewel
Wild strawberry
Sun sparks merriment
Crystal laughter of flowers
Jewelbilent.

———————

Peonies   Chris Moran

Peonies
candy floss
coloured pompoms prepare
for a summer parade
Cheerleaders.

Autumn Leaves   Chris Moran

Leaves
grow old
with gentle acceptance
that they will eventually
fall.

———————

Hidden

Mist
thin veil
hiding the garden
all will be revealed
later.

———————

Decision

Golden
snow falls
from the trees
Autumn has decided to
settle.

———————

Soul Strength   Elaine Patricia Morris

Sparkly
Crystal diamonds
Suspended on silk.
Spider's webs amaze me.
Water.

Bubbles

Elaine Patricia Morris

Rainbow
iridescent, fragile
spectrum of light.
We dip and wave.
Bubbles.

———————

Dreams

Kathy Uyen Nguyen

foggy
spring morning
looking for you
in dreams but always
lost.

———————

Butterfly

coral
dewdropped sky
a butterfly skips
across this journal page
wordless.

———————

Elfje Variant

Rosemary Nissen-Wade

Oh!
winter flowers
pink and white
like delicate Spring blossoms –
frangipani.

Bluebells   JulesPaige

bluebells
silent ring
heard in dreams
pastel lilt lingering still
dainty.

————————

Walking

walking
seeking shade
the winding path
slowed his breath into
sleep.

————————

Winter

snow
cold flakes
on my eyelashes
freezing my dreams of
spring.

————————

Rain   Freya Pickard

hissing
rushing, pouring
blurring office windows
streaming off tarmac roads;
Rain.

Poplar

Freya Pickard

silver
undersides flash
quiver, shake, flicker,
darkness alternates with paleness;
poplar.

———

Wolf Mist

gloaming
wolf mist
hunkers low, trailing
purposefully, lit by waning
moon.

———

Underestimated

Ina Schroders-Zeeders

Underestimated
your power
I give in
this has to be
love.

———

Blue Jewels

Evi Schumacher

Lapis
blue jewels
one two three
flitting branch to branch
Bluebirds.

Shadow   Evi Schumacher

Shadow
silent flight
golden eyes glow
magic in the grove
Owl.

————

Autumn's Arrival   Rachel Tapping

Suddenly
the evenings
turn to dusk.
There's no turning back.
Autumn.

————

Evening Light

Evening.
The moment
before the sun
gracefully takes her leave.
Beauty!

————

Concerto   Jo Young

Tchaikovsky's
violin concerto
prances in sunshine.
Sky blue dancing joy
encapsulated.

Elfje in the orignal Dutch and in translation:

65

Tulips   Catherine van Vliet-Saivres

Onbevangen
De Tulpen
Ze groeien gestadig.
Ik zie het gabeuren.
Vrij!

Detached
The tulips
Steady they grow.
I see it happen.
Free!

———————

The Sea

Blauw
De Zee
Ze komt, gaat.
Aeonen lang weet ze.
Bewust…

Blue
The sea
It comes, goes.
For aeons it knows.
Aware…

Acknowledgements:

I would like to thank all those poets, writers and bloggers who have shared the Elfje journey with me, in particular those whose work is represented in these pages.

A special thank you to Catherine van Vliet-Saivres for introducing me to the Elfje form as well as for her contributions in the original Dutch, and also to the family of the late Cynthia Jobin for permission to include her work here.

Finally a big thank you to my husband for his unfailing support and encouragement, not to mention all the cups of tea and coffee!